CAREER AS AN

INVESTMENT FUND MANAGER

Financial Analyst

Hedge Fund Manager

THE CAREER YOU CHOOSE NOW WILL have a big effect on the rest of your life, determining things like where you will live, who you will spend your time with and, obviously, how much money you will make. This is a very important decision and deserves to be taken seriously. The fact that you are taking the time to read this report says you are probably on the right track.

Making money is an important part of any career. Even if money is not your primary motivation, it is important because it will allow you to do the things you want to do, whether it is something optional like take a nice vacation or something dutiful like pay the rent or send a child to college.

Helping other people to make money is a great way to make your own. Investment fund managers create the products that regular people invest their money in to make more money. Their work is central to the life-planning process of millions of people. Investment fund managers help people to save for retirement, to buy homes, send their kids to college and achieve financial freedom. Without them, most people would simply stash their money in a bank and earn a tiny rate of interest. Investment fund managers help people to put their money to work.

Demand for investment fund managers is always healthy, although in recent years computers have started to do more of the work once assigned to humans. Most investors, however, want to know that a real person is at the helm of their investment vehicles, making trained professionals more important than ever. Investment fund managers are the brains behind a variety of investments, including mutual funds, exchange-traded funds, hedge funds and private equity funds. For the most part, investment fund managers work behind the scenes and rarely meet the people who buy their products. Portfolio managers do the same work, but usually for private clients. The best fund managers achieve actual star power in the investment world and their reputations help to sell their products.

WHAT YOU CAN DO NOW

THERE ARE PLENTY OF WAYS TO LEARN about this career right now. Pay close attention to the financial markets. Step one for an aspiring investment fund manager is to stay on top of the market. "The market" actually refers to many distinct markets where financial products are bought and sold. The most important markets in the United States are the New York Stock Exchange and the Nasdaq Stock Market ("Nasdaq" was originally an acronym for National Association of Securities Dealers Automated Quotations). Less well-known but also important are the Chicago Mercantile Exchange and Chicago Board of Trade. American investors also have to pay attention to major foreign markets, including the

Shanghai Stock Exchange, London Stock Exchange, Deutsche Börse and Bombay Stock Exchange. It is easy to follow all of these markets and more on the internet. Check in on them every day. That is what you will do as an investment fund manager.

Investment fund managers also never stop learning about their business. The stakes are extremely high and every little tidbit of knowledge helps fund managers to stay ahead of the markets and ahead of their competitors. There is no lack of books, magazines, websites, newsletters, blogs, and subscription services available to tell you everything about making money in the markets. You must read The Wall Street Journal, and look into Kiplinger's, Investor's Business Daily, Bloomberg, and Money.

After you have spent some time following the markets and learning about investing, give it a try yourself. You can open a brokerage account with many online brokerages for as little as $1000. Some offer educational programs where you can invest play money and see how you do. This is an excellent way to start. Most online brokerages also provide tools and databases to help investors find the right investment vehicles for their needs and their tolerance for risk. You should start by risking some of your own money before you take on someone else's.

HISTORY OF THE CAREER

INVESTMENT FUNDS AS WE KNOW THEM today are a relatively new innovation, but investing has been around for a very long time. The basic concept of investing capital in a company or project in the hope of making more money has not changed much at all. It is the number of options available to investors that has vastly increased.

The earliest investments were only available to the wealthy. Go back far enough, to the dawn of agrarian society about 10,000 years ago, and the only wealth that mattered was land. Everybody needed land to live on and to grow food, so owning land was extremely important. In early societies, only leaders were allowed to own land. Kings, emperors and pharaohs, for example, were considered the legal owners of their realms. Their subjects were merely allowed to live there. Favored subjects who provided exceptional service to the ruler were awarded with titles of nobility and tracts of land, thereby creating their own small realms.

The growth of city-states in the years on both sides of the Common Era expanded investment opportunities, but not by much. The wealthy used their capital to establish businesses and invited other investors to join them. In return for making an investment, investors were entitled to a share of the profit – or loss – from the business. The history of investing from then until now is concerned primarily with making investment opportunities available to more and more people.

By the year 1000 or so, a merchant class had arisen to join the aristocrats and rulers. The merchant class was composed of astute entrepreneurs who had built successful businesses and had risen through the ranks of society to establish themselves as an entirely new social class one step below the titled aristocrats and one step above the masses of common people. The slow expansion of the merchant class into the modern middle class is an important thread in the history of the Western world. By the Renaissance period, roughly 1200-1500, merchants had built globe-spanning trading empires and established modern institutions like banks and credit systems.

It should be pointed out that the wealthy had employed financial specialists for centuries to help them manage their money. While these advisors were arguably portfolio managers, their portfolios tended to be composed of relatively few classes of assets and owned by one person or family. This was very different from the portfolio managers and fund managers of today, who generally serve many clients and keep track of portfolios including hundreds or even thousands of investments.

The first financial exchange was established in the Dutch city of Antwerp in 1531. It allowed investors to gather and share information about investments. Within a few years the first joint-stock companies were founded. Among the most famous of these were the British East India Company (1600) and the Dutch East India Company (1602), both created to fund exploration and commercial ventures in newly discovered lands a long way from Europe. These joint-stock companies established several important principles, including transparent ownership, limited liability for share owners (boards of directors and company officers held all liability), permanence of existence, and transferability of possession of shares. The Amsterdam Stock Exchange, generally considered to be the world's first, grew out of the Dutch East India Company, which issued paper stock certificates to its shareholders.

Although the basic principles of investing had been established, the world of finance was still dominated by the wealthy. In 1772 a Dutch financier named Abraham van Ketwich created the first investment fund that aimed to sell shares to small investors. His fund, called Eendragt Maakt Magt ("Unity Creates Strength") was a success and opened the door for people of modest means to enter sophisticated financial markets.

The first mutual fund was opened in the United States in 1924. Called the Massachusetts Investors Trust, it still exists today. The fund bought shares of stock in many companies and then sold shares in the fund, allowing small investors to benefit from owning many more stocks than they could afford if they had to buy them one at a time. The model was a winner with investors, and by the 1970s more than $50 billion was invested in mutual funds in the United States alone.

Mutual funds not only offer small investors an easy way to diversify their investments, they also help to spread risk among many companies and industries, making them popular with large institutional investors like pension funds that need to be able to mitigate risk over very long periods of time. Index funds are especially popular when it comes to mitigating risk. A mutual fund that mimics the entire return of the Standard and Poor 500 – an index of the 500 largest publicly traded companies – helps to insulate investors from drops in specific industries by spreading capital to every industry in the index. Today, investors can find mutual funds catering to just about any industry, interest, or tolerance for risk. About $20 trillion is invested in mutual funds in the United States today.

Exchange-traded funds (ETFs) are similar to mutual funds in many respects. They also represent a diversified portfolio of investment vehicles and can be purchased one share at a time. They differ from mutual funds, however, in that they can be traded in real-time just like stocks. Mutual funds are purchased at the end of the trading day, giving everybody who put in an order that day exactly the same price. Mutual funds also tend to have more complex fee structures than ETFs. ETFs also tend to offer investors better liquidity over mutual funds, although this is not always the case with ETFs devoted to very narrow market strategies.

Hedge funds are very specialized investment funds that make liberal use of derivatives and leverage in order to make money. Hedge funds are very actively managed, usually by multiple fund managers. Generally speaking, hedge funds are open only to accredited investors and may come with restrictions like a prohibition on selling shares within the first year of ownership. An accredited investor is defined by the federal government as anybody who has earned at least $200,000 per year in each of the last three years – $300,000 for married couples – or who has a net worth of at least $1,000,000. Especially risky or complex investments are often restricted to accredited investors because it is assumed that they know what they are doing. Hedge funds also typically require very large initial investments of at least $100,000 and often much more.

Investment fund managers are needed to manage all of these funds. They are also needed to look after portfolios maintained by wealthy individuals, corporations, institutions and government entities like pension funds.

WHERE YOU WILL WORK

AS AN INVESTMENT FUND MANAGER you will eventually be able to work pretty much anywhere you want, but that may not be until later in your career. There is no question that New York is the capital of American finance, and Chicago is the runner-up. The internet, however, has freed fund managers from geography and nowadays fund managers can be found everywhere.

The solid majority of investment fund managers work in New York City, America's largest city and its financial center. Another large cohort calls the Windy City home. As an aspiring investment fund manager you could aim to build a career in either of these places. There are more jobs there than anywhere else, but it must be said that there is also more competition. Even if you have no desire to live in either New York or Chicago for the long term, you may spend a few years of your career in one or the other of those cities. In fact, it can be argued that you probably should aim for at least an internship in New York or Chicago, and maybe even your first job after college. As few as three to five years in either of these cities could serve you well for the rest of your career.

Not everybody opts for the capitals of finance. The most successful fund manager of all time, Warren Buffet, has spent most of his career in his hometown of Omaha, Nebraska. He finished his formal education in New York, at Columbia University and the New York Institute of Finance, and worked in the city for a few years as an investment salesman. He returned to Omaha in his early 20s, however, and has been there ever since. His company, Berkshire Hathaway, is now the largest financial service company in the world. Shares in the company are also the most expensive in the world, at roughly $300,000 *per share*, as of 2018.

The profusion of internet-enabled databases and trading platforms has made geography less important for fund managers. There are mutual fund companies across the country, including hedge funds, exchange- traded funds and private-equity funds. Get some experience first and you ought to be able to get a job just about anywhere you want. After a decade or so in the business you may even want to consider starting your own company. Take a hard look at the mutual fund pages on a brokerage website and you will see that every fund lists the name of its principal manager. The best fund managers build reputations that take them to the top of the profession. They become financial stars.

DESCRIPTION OF WORK DUTIES

Financial Analysts

Financial analysts are careerists in the early stages of their careers who are not yet fund managers. Almost nobody comes straight out of college and into a position as a fund manager. Most careerists work as financial analysts in some capacity before moving into management.

Financial analysts are responsible for analyzing all manner of financial data. This can include financial data on specific companies, like return on investment, past stock performance, profit or loss, revenue, earnings per share, and the rate of a company's growth in recent years. Financial analysts also look at items of importance to specific companies, like subscriber growth for a publishing company or how many new stores a hot new franchise company has opened in the past year or two. They will also look at one-time events that affect the company's bottom line, like the results of a lawsuit, a patent award, a real estate sale, or the retirement of an important executive. All of these items factors into financial analysis of a company.

Financial analysts also take into account the prevailing winds of the economy. They track the ups and downs of stock markets around the world. They look into currency fluctuations and the political events that may be triggering them. Wars and natural disasters can have huge short-term effects on the health of a company or even entire industries. In the fast-moving technological world of today, financial analysts also have to be wary of new innovations that could revolutionize or threaten the existence of entire industries.

Financial analysts generally prepare detailed reports of their findings and send them to clients and managers who use their reports to make financial decisions. Financial analysts work for mutual funds, exchange-traded funds, hedge funds, closed-end funds, private portfolios, institutions, companies with money to invest and wealthy individuals. They also work in media, offering their analysis to readers or viewers.

Analysts are sometimes classified as buy-side or sell-side analysts. Buy-side analysts generally work for funds and other entities that have money to invest. They devise investment strategies for their clients or employers. Sell-side analysts prepare reports to be used by financial advisors and financial sales agents who then use that information to sell investment vehicles to their clients.

Financial analysts usually have a specialty or two. A specialty can be a specific industry or technology, like consumer staples or information security. It can also be a specific country or region. The financial market is global, and even retail investors – individuals – have access to markets around the world. There are financial analysts devoted to a single country, like India, a fast-growing financial market; and to entire regions, like Europe, which is a very mature market.

Mutual Fund and Exchange-Traded Fund Managers

When most people think about investment fund managers they think of the dedicated careerists who manage mutual funds and exchange-traded funds. That's because just about everybody owns shares in a mutual fund or ETF, even if indirectly through a company savings plan or retirement plan like a 401(k).

Mutual funds and ETFs have essentially the same goal: To provide investors with greater exposure to more investments than they could get by investing on their own. There are differences between them – most notably ETFs can be traded like stocks and mutual funds cannot. An S&P 500 ETF, for example, owns shares in all 500 companies represented in the S&P 500. Creating such a portfolio on your own would be expensive and difficult. With an ETF, it is easy.

Most mutual funds and ETFs use a theme or index to guide their investments. A theme can be mathematical, like investing only in companies with small market capitalizations, or a more expansive idea, like only investing in companies whose policies meet certain religious or social criteria. There are mutual funds devoted to specific countries and regions of the world, specific industries and specific technologies, just to name a few. Many funds and ETFs are also linked to specific indexes, like the Dow Jones Industrial Index or the S&P 500. There are also many indexes you have probably never heard of, like the Shiller Barclays CAPE US Sector Index or the United States Copper Index. In all cases, funds tied to indexes attempt to replicate the performance of the entire index within their fund, making it easy for investors to have exposure to many more investment vehicles than they could manage on their own. Index funds tied to broad indexes like the Dow Jones or the NASDAQ also tend to mitigate risk because they spread investments across a wide range of companies and industries.

Mutual fund managers and ETF managers must aim to maximize return on their investments within the parameters of the fund's stated objective. Investors who put their money into an ETF promising exposure to growth stocks in India trust that their fund manager will do exactly that. To make these decisions fund managers generally rely on input from financial analysts. In major fund companies most of the financial analysis is done in-house by armies of financial analysts. In smaller firms, much of the analysis may be purchased from outside firms. Either way, it is up to mutual fund and ETF managers to make the best decisions on behalf of their clients.

Fund managers in the mutual fund and ETF industries are the ones who sometimes become financial world celebrities. Look at the information page for any fund and you will find the name of the manager and the date he or she started managing the fund. Most of the names will be unknown to you, but some of them are very well-known within the profession. A few are even well--known to ordinary investors. These managers can name their price when they take over a fund.

Portfolio Managers

All investment fund managers are ultimately portfolio managers. Investment funds, whether they are called mutual funds, ETFs or something else, are all portfolios of investments. The title portfolio manager, however, most often refers to an investment fund manager who manages a portfolio for a specific entity, like a business, institution, family or wealthy individual.

A portfolio manager for a wealthy individual, for example, takes charge of managing that person's investment portfolio. Such a portfolio would likely include stocks, mutual funds, ETFs, real estate and maybe some exotic investments like hedge funds, art and antiques. A portfolio manager probably would not be in charge of buying and selling art and antiques – there are other experts for that – but would definitely keep track of their value and how they fit into their client's overall portfolio. A portfolio manager for a wealthy family provides similar services for family estates, managing assets owned by the family or family trust and making sure that the financial needs of all family members are met.

Institutions like universities, think tanks and charities need portfolio managers to augment the revenue they receive from grants and donations. A typical charity, for example, would not last very long if it had to meet its expenses only with revenue generated by donations. Universities use the income generated by their portfolios to underwrite scholarship programs and bring down the cost of tuition.

Businesses also hire portfolio managers to manage their investments. Successful companies maintain a ready pool of capital to use for emergencies or to fund special projects. Very successful companies like Apple and Microsoft maintain reserves of billions of dollars. Oddly, those reserves are often known as "cash reserves." Some of that money is undoubtedly kept in cash, but most of it is invested. Money is a tool to accomplish things. For a business, money is capital to fund the next product. If money has to sit around for a while, it should generate income.

Hedge Fund Managers

A relatively recent addition to the world of investment funds, hedge funds have generated substantial interest from investors for their ability to make huge amounts of money – sometimes. Hedge funds can invest in literally anything. Hedge fund managers have to be smart, resourceful and fearless. So do hedge fund investors.

Hedge funds are only open to accredited investors – investors with a net worth of at least $1 million or income of at least $200,000 in each of the last two years – and usually have very high minimum investments out of reach of the average investor. Hedge funds often use risky investment vehicles like derivatives, currencies and venture capital schemes. They also tend to employ extreme leverage – borrowing money in order to make investments. Most hedge funds require investors to leave their money in the fund for a set number of years before they can take it out. This is great when the fund is making money. It is not so great when investors watch their investments shrink and there is nothing they can do about it.

Hedge fund managers are very well compensated. A typical fee structure is known as "two and twenty." Under this plan, hedge fund managers are paid two percent of the value of the assets plus 20 percent of the profits earned in a year. So the manager of a $100 million hedge fund will be paid a minimum of $2 million – two percent of the value of the fund – even if the fund does not make any money. If this hypothetical $100 million fund makes 30 percent, or $30 million, the manager would be entitled to another $6 million, or 20 percent of the profit. In terms of compensation, hedge fund managers are at the top of the fund-management business.

STORIES OF INVESTMENT MANAGERS

I Am a Portfolio Manager for a Pension Fund

"Everybody depends upon portfolio managers, whether they know it or not. People who automatically put money into an Individual Retirement Account depend upon portfolio managers, and so do people who own mutual funds and ETFs. But nobody depends upon portfolios managers as much as people who are vested in a pension. We hold their retirement years in the palm of our hands.

There are two kinds of pension plans: defined-benefit plans and defined-contribution plans. Most people nowadays contribute to defined-contribution plans. That is, they contribute a defined amount of money to the plan on a regular basis – usually monthly – and their employers often make additional contributions. Nobody knows what the plan will be worth at the time of retirement. Portfolio managers just do their best to maximize earnings and appreciation of principle.

A defined-benefit plan is different. In this case, benefits are guaranteed decades in advance. Most people who receive defined-benefit pensions are government employees because only governments exist in perpetuity. The state pension I work for, for example, will never go out of business because it is part of the state government. A regular business couldn't possibly guarantee that it will be around, say, 40 years from now but a state government will be.

My job is to choose investments for our pension fund. In that sense, I am a portfolio manager like any other. I choose investments that I think will grow and provide the growth needed to meet our pension obligations to the state's retirees. Our retirees depend upon me in their golden years. We are talking about people in their 60s and older. They fulfilled their side of the bargain by working for the state for several decades, and now it's the state's turn to honor its side of the deal.

I also have an obligation to the taxpayers of the state. If I don't manage the pension fund well, and come up short, it's the taxpayers who will have to make up the difference, and they won't be very happy about it. I figure that I'm doing my job well if most taxpayers don't even know I exist.

State pension funds run some of the largest investment funds in the world. The California Public Employees Retirement System, or CalPERS, for example, is the largest public pension fund in the United States. It is so big that it can influence major corporate decisions simply by threatening to sell a company's stock if it doesn't take steps CalPERS deems necessary. My state's pension fund is nowhere near as large but we still have influence.

I have a Master of Science degree in finance, and several licenses and certifications. I have been in this business for a long time. I rely upon a number of financial analysts specializing in all areas of stocks, bonds, real estate and other investment specialties. Together we have done a good job of meeting our obligations to our retirees and our taxpayers."

I Am a Financial Analyst for a Mutual Fund Company

"My job is to provide the fund managers at my company with ideas for our family of mutual funds. I perform extremely detailed research on stocks in companies that fit a particular fund's profile, prepare reports and send them to the fund managers so they can decide whether or not to buy the stocks for the funds they manage.

I got into this work for many reasons. I am fascinated by the intricacies of business and how different companies in completely different industries can ultimately be compared on the basis of their financial performance alone. I guess you could say I'm good with numbers, because that's what this job is all about.

I always knew that I wanted to major in business in college but I wasn't sure exactly where I wanted to go. I majored in business administration because it gave me a broad overview of the world of business and helped me to find my own way. I spent a few years after college working for a large consulting firm. It was in that job that I found my way to finance. Finance allows companies to grow, invest in themselves and attract investors. So I earned an MBA with a concentration in finance, and earned my CFA certification – that's Chartered Financial Analyst – and started working as an equities analyst for my current employer.

Fund managers select the investments that go into our mutual funds, but they only select investments from the pool of ideas that my colleagues and I present to them. This is a very large company, and we have hundreds of equities analysts on our staff. We all specialize in relatively narrow areas so that we can focus our research and become the true experts that our company and clients need.

My specialty is new internet companies. You may think that the internet has been gobbled up by giants like Google and Amazon, but there is a constant stream of up-and-comers out there who are looking to make their mark. My job is to figure out which of these upstarts will have enough staying power to be worth investing in. I look at these companies from all possible angles. I look into how much capital they had to start up, who gave it to them, how many shares they have issued and who bought them. I look into their nuts-and-bolts financial performance, including their sales, revenue, profits and every other statistic I can think of. Then I look into larger trends in the industry and see where the new company fits into the market. It can take weeks to thoroughly research a single company. When I'm done, I write a report and send it to the fund managers who may or may not choose to buy shares in the company.

I'd like to become a fund manager myself someday. Being an equities analyst first isn't absolutely necessary, but I'm glad I'm starting out at this level because I'm learning all of the tricks of the trade. I plan to go far in this business."

I Am a Portfolio Manager for a Private University

"You might be surprised at how much money universities and other institutions are sitting on. Most people look at an institution like a university and see tuition fees as the main source of revenue, but that's not really the case, especially at private universities that don't depend upon state funding. We have to generate our own revenue from within, too.

Like most people, I started out in this business as a financial analyst. I worked my way up to fund management at a major mutual fund company where I served on the management teams of several mutual funds and ETFs over the years. I have a master's degree in finance and CFA certification, too. I've been in this business for a long time.

I joined the university's staff because I saw it as a challenge. This university has a portfolio worth hundreds of millions of dollars. The portfolio accomplishes many things. It provides the university with a fund to get through hard times, emergencies and unexpected drops in enrollment. It subsidizes many of the university's expenses, from maintenance of the campus, to paying professors, to underwriting research projects. Most importantly, the portfolio supports many of our scholarship programs. We could never cover all of these expenses on tuition fees and alumni donations alone.

Most of the portfolio is invested in the stock market. Just like other retail investors, we own stocks, mutual funds and ETFs. They provide us with the kind of liquidity we need to cover expenses as they happen. We can always sell stock to come up with some cash. We also own bonds to limit our risk exposure. Our portfolio also includes significant real estate holdings, which tend to be relatively stable and a good store of value, even if they aren't very liquid. Anybody who has ever tried to sell a house will tell you that you can't unload real estate overnight.

Our portfolio comes with a few restrictions that don't apply to most other funds or portfolios. The university administration requires me to invest a large portion of our assets in investment vehicles that promote values espoused by the university. I can't put our money into alcohol or tobacco stocks, for example, or into funds that do business in certain politically unpalatable countries. This is a pretty common arrangement for institutional portfolio management, although the rules differ from one institution to the next.

I love this career because every day is a challenge. I look over a complex basket of investment vehicles and determine which ones are performing as expected and which ones aren't. I sell off the ones that aren't working out, and then make a plan to replace them. It's a fascinating, never-ending process. Have you ever taken pride in watching a garden grow? That's how I feel about our portfolio."

I Am a Mutual Fund Manager

"I am the person most people think of when they think of an investment fund manager. Americans have trillions of dollars invested in mutual funds. Most people have money in mutual funds even if they don't know it. Pension funds and 401(k) retirement plans invest in mutual funds, for example.

I always knew that I wanted to manage mutual funds. After earning a bachelor's degree in business administration I spent a few years selling mutual funds, ETFs and stocks to retail investors. I quickly discovered that people like to invest in mutual funds for two reasons: people like to know that a team of professionals is managing their money for them. Second, many people really get into themes. So I earned an MBA in finance and a CFA certification so I could get behind the scenes in the mutual fund business.

Mutual funds employ teams of experts to achieve their stated goals. If you think a particular industry is destined for growth you can buy stocks in that industry and try to manage them yourself, or you can buy a mutual fund devoted to that industry and let a team of experts manage them for you. A mutual fund can also own dozens or even hundreds of different stocks while most retail investors can only afford to own a handful.

Themes are important. The most important reason is that a tightly focused investment objective, or theme, establishes expectations for both investors and fund managers. A mutual fund that says it will invest in mid-cap growth stocks from everywhere in Asia except Japan – a common theme – gives both sides of the equation: a benchmark and a way ahead.

The truth is that most fund managers have a tough time beating the market at least 50 percent of the time. This sounds terrible but the truth is a little more complicated. The experts sell poorly performing stocks and replace them with new ones far more often than most retail investors do. Sooner or later this churn delivers a winning streak that retail investors just can't match. Can you choose your own stocks and make money along the way? Yes, but for most people it will take too much time and effort on their part. When you buy a mutual fund you hire experts like me to make those choices for you. Over time, we'll almost certainly make more money for you, too."

PERSONAL QUALIFICATIONS

TO SUCCEED IN THIS CAREER YOU MUST HAVE A genuine talent and love for mathematics. Investment fund management is all about numbers. Some investment vehicles are likely to do better than others. Nobody has a crystal ball, however, so financial predictions have to be made mostly on the basis of numbers. Investment fund managers spend most of their time analyzing the past performance of potential investment vehicles and then trying to forecast how they are likely to do in the future based on the current economic climate and forecasts. This involves manipulating numbers using extremely complex formulas and algorithms.

You should be absolutely confident in your computer skills. If you think investment websites aimed at regular investors offer complicated computer tools, you will not believe the techniques professionals use. Enter your numbers for parameters like debt-to-equity, earnings per share, price-to-earnings or any other data you can come up with, and then test your prognostications backwards using historical data and forwards using the latest forecasts. These professional-grade tools generally require costly subscriptions to databases and analysis services in order to yield the best answers. All of your competitors will have access to the same tools, which means it is incumbent upon you to offer something different to your customers: your insight and intuition.

It is easy to say that this career requires excellent

analytical skills. That means not just being able to crunch numbers and look at forecasts, but being able to do so without emotion or bias. A common fallacy is investing in something for emotional reasons rather than logical ones. Many people invest in companies they know and like. This is a terrible investment strategy because it ignores the math behind the investment. You may love the company, but if the math does not support it, you should not invest in it.

ATTRACTIVE FEATURES

FIRST AND FOREMOST IS OBVIOUSLY the money. Investment fund managers can make a great deal of money. Finance is one of the few industries in which employees – as opposed to owners and entrepreneurs – can earn millions of dollars. Many investment fund managers start their careers with $100,000 annual salaries plus bonuses for meeting or exceeding performance targets. Managers who do their jobs well can expect to earn much more money as the years go by. Keep in mind, however, that this steady rise in income does not happen automatically. Investment fund managers are judged by their performance. Many people get rich in this business but only by consistently doing better than everybody else.

Making money for yourself is great, but so is making money for other people. Investment fund managers rarely work directly with clients. Financial advisors handle relations with the people who actually buy funds. It is not unusual for investment fund managers to spend a few years as financial advisors early in their careers, however, so there is some overlap in how they conduct their business. Still, investment fund managers are responsible for creating and managing investment vehicles that enable regular people to build their net worth and achieve their dreams. A regular savings account at a bank might earn as little as one percent in annual interest. A good mutual fund might make 10 to 15 percent. In a really good year a fund might make 30 percent or more. For people saving their money to do important things like buy a house or send a child to college, the difference is very important. A $10,000 investment in a bank account at one percent per year will be worth about $11,000 after 10 years. The same $10,000 investment in a mutual fund averaging 10 percent a year will be worth almost $26,000 after the same amount of time. You will be able to make that happen for thousands of fortunate investors.

Finance is what makes the world go 'round. Finance bankrolls the companies that create the jobs. Finance generates transactions that pay taxes. Finance provides funding for scientific research, scholarship funds, and every charitable cause on earth. Investment fund managers are an important part of the financial world. Your decisions will affect the lives of countless people. You will also find yourself going to philanthropic galas and frequenting the first-class lounges at airports.

UNATTRACTIVE ASPECTS

INVESTMENT FUND MANAGERS MAY HAVE very high earnings and plenty of opportunities to help other people achieve their dreams, but there is a definite downside to a career in investment fund management. The competition is daunting, and does not stop after you get your foot in the door. It should come as no surprise that many people would like to become investment fund managers. Competition for jobs is quite keen and it only gets worse as you move up the ladder. Major fund companies hire financial analysts straight out of graduate school, but only a handful make it to the top. The competition is mostly based on the numbers. The financial analysts who rise to the top do so because they achieve better results than their peers. There is no getting around this basic fact. If you want to become an investment fund manager you will have to be on top of your game every single day.

The margin for error in this business is very, very low. Either you are beating the market and your competitors, or you are not. Click "sell" a little too late or too soon and you could lose millions of dollars. If you put a big bet on a new stock by buying a large position for your fund and then lose money you could ruin your reputation in the industry, especially if the buy was a risky one in the first place. This business rewards risk-takers when they succeed and punishes them when they fail. Nonetheless, everybody continues to take big risks because that is where the biggest rewards are.

When industries wane, businesses fail and regular people go broke, many people reflexively point the finger at the financial industry as the culprit. With very few exceptions, this is not really true. The financial industry is hardly at fault when consumers stop demanding something. In fact, financial professionals are likely to be the first to sound the alarm when an industry is starting to struggle. They are the ones doing the math. Onlookers with an emotional investment in a dying industry may not want to believe the numbers, but financial analysts always do.

EDUCATION AND TRAINING

INVESTMENT FUND MANAGERS NEED EXCELLENT education and credentials before they can enter the workforce. If you plan to enter this career you will need to set your sights on earning a graduate degree in finance.

You can take one of many paths to get there, however. First, you will have to earn an undergraduate degree. Financial professionals most often major in finance, economics, accounting or business administration.

Business administration programs tend to be well-rounded curricula that expose students to all of the business basics, including accounting, finance, marketing, management, economics, business law and an array of related subjects.

Bachelor's degrees in finance concentrate on subjects like banking, investment theory, financial management and risk management.

Economics degrees cover such topics as microeconomics, macroeconomics and statistics.

Accounting is the mathematical bottom line of business, so accounting majors take classes in subjects like auditing, tax accounting and computerized information systems.

Any of these majors will get you pointed in the right direction for a career as an investment fund manager, especially if you spend a few years in the workforce before you pursue a master's degree.

Eventually you will need to earn a master's degree in

finance. There are many programs to choose from, with some offering a Master of Science degree in finance, and others offering a Master of Business Administration degree (MBA) with a concentration in finance. Such programs typically require students to take courses in advanced economics and accounting, quantitative methods, financial modeling, corporate finance, and portfolio management.

Do not pass up the opportunity to complete an internship while you are an undergraduate. Most internships are paid and many come with special programs not available to regular employees, like seminars with senior leadership or opportunities to work in different departments during your internship. Many new careerists land their first job after college with the company where they did their internship. Other aspiring careerists discover during an internship that their dream career is not what they thought it would be and change their majors when they get back to school. Either way, you will never have a better opportunity to explore a career for a few months and then walk away without burning your bridges behind you. You will make excellent connections and learn things you cannot possibly be taught in a classroom.

Investment fund managers and portfolio managers must be licensed and/or certified. Regulations vary from state to state and from one company to the next depending upon the exact requirements of particular jobs. There are many licenses and certifications available to financial professionals. The two that are most important to fund managers are the Chartered Financial Analyst designation offered by the CFA Institute and the Series 65 license. The CFA designation can be earned after passing all three levels of the CFA Program, each of which requires a six-hour exam.

The Series 65 license is awarded after passing a test called the Uniform Investment Adviser Law Examination, which is written by the North American Securities Administrators Association and administered by the Financial Industry Regulatory Authority, or FINRA. The test consists of 130 multiple-choice questions and must be completed in three hours.

You may also have to earn a Series 3 license if you get into trading futures or commodities. The Series 3 exam is written by the National Futures Association and is also administered by FINRA. There are a number of other license and certifications to be earned if your career path demands them.

EARNINGS

INVESTMENT FUND MANAGERS GET PAID very well. Their role in helping people to make money is what really counts.

Financial analysts straight out of college can expect to earn $50,000 to $70,000 per year with an MBA. Graduates of very elite programs can earn much more. Investment fund managers and careerists with similar titles like portfolio managers can easily break the $100,000 mark after they have a few years of experience, and many financial managers command salaries of $150,000 or more. Salaries for senior executives who take on leadership responsibilities can top $200,000 per year.

Hedge fund managers are at the top of the profession, with compensation that can reach into the millions.

Many fund and portfolio managers are also paid bonuses based on their performance. These bonuses can vary widely from one firm to the next and can add anywhere from a few thousand dollars to a few million dollars to your annual earnings.

A few investment fund managers rise to the level of financial superstars. Putting their names on a fund attracts customers, and investment fund companies know it. These hardworking few can earn millions of dollars per year in salary and bonuses. There is only one way to climb into this rank: Beat the market, year after year after year.

You should also keep in mind the fact that if you become an investment fund manager you will probably do quite well with your own investments. Like most people, you will buy stocks, mutual funds, exchange-traded funds, bonds and other investment vehicles, often taking positions on the same securities that you are recommending to your clients.

OPPORTUNITIES

DEMAND FOR FINANCIAL PROFESSIONALS is expected to grow by more than 10 percent over the next decade, which is higher than most occupations. This is due to several reasons. First, demand rises in line with the state of the overall economy. When the economy grows, so does demand for financial professionals. Second, there are more investment vehicles than ever before, and everybody from regular consumers to giant corporations needs expertise to choose among them. Finally, the world of finance has never been more accessible than it is today. With a few clicks of a mouse anybody in the world can get the scoop on almost any financial product – and then decide that they need professional help to sort it all out. All of these factors bode well for you as an aspiring investment fund manager.

Competition for such interesting, high-paying jobs will

always be keen, however, and you owe it to yourself to stay ahead of the pack if you want to move up in the world. Seek out opportunities to earn new credentials. The CFA Institute, for example, offers certifications beyond the Chartered Financial Analyst designation. Earn them and add them to your résumé. Other professional associations offer additional credentials you should look into. Show potential employers – and clients – that you are on top of the financial world by keeping your résumé up-to-date.

Your goal may be to become an investment fund manager, but nobody starts out as an investment fund manager. You will probably hold several titles before you reach your goal, like financial analyst, financial advisor and portfolio manager. Your titles may include words like associate or assistant. Be willing to zig and zag a bit on your way to your goal of becoming an investment fund manager. Broad experience in the financial industry will serve you well when the time comes to make the big decisions as a manager.

GETTING STARTED

SO YOU HAVE FINISHED COLLEGE, EARNED YOUR FIRST few financial certifications and are ready to step out into the real world. Congratulations! Get your personal marketing materials in order, contact everybody you have ever met in the financial business and keep an open mind.

The first thing you need to do is prepare a top-notch résumé. This is your single-most important personal marketing document. If you are unsure of your own résumé-writing skills, there are plenty of books and software applications that can help you. Your college outplacement office may also offer résumé-writing services. Many of the jobs for which you will apply will require you to build your résumé in online applications. If you have to spend some money to get a polished résumé, do it.

Send your résumé to everybody you know in the financial business. Start with the company with whom you completed an internship. Include former college professors, friends who are a few years ahead of you in the business, and anybody else you can think of who may be able to point you in the right direction. Most jobs are filled by word-of-mouth. Former finance professors probably do not have jobs to offer you but they may know somebody who does.

Most of all, keep an open mind. Almost nobody lands their dream job straight out of college. You probably do not really know what your dream job is. Get your foot in the door, get some professional experience and then take a look at where you want to go and what you want to do. You may be amazed at how much you will learn and grow in a few short years. Take every chance you get. Good luck!

ASSOCIATIONS, PERIODICALS, WEBSITES

■ **Association of Certified International Investment Analysts**
www.aciia.org

■ **Association for Financial Professionals**
www.afponline.org

■ **Association to Advance Collegiate Schools of Business**
www.aacsb.edu

■ **Barron's**
www.barrons.com

■ **Bloomberg**
www.bloomberg.com

■ **Calculator.net**
www.calculator.net

■ **CFA Institute**
www.cfainstitute.org

■ **Chartered Alternative Investment Association**
www.caia.org

■ **CNBC**
www.cnbc.com

■ **Financewalk**
www.financewalk.com

■ **Financial Industry Regulatory Authority**
www.finra.org

■ **Forbes**
www.forbes.com

- **Institute for Financial Literacy**
  www.financiallit.org

- **International Research Association**
  www.lifaexam.org

- **Investopedia**
  www.investopedia.com

- **Investors Business Daily**
  www.investors.com

- **Kiplinger's**
  www.kiplinger.com

- **MarketWatch**
  www.marketwatch.com

- **MBA Programs**
  www.mbaprograms.org

- **Money Magazine**
  www.time.com/money

- **Money Morning**
  www.moneymorning.com

- **Motif**
  www.motifinvesting.com

- **Motley Fool**
  www.motleyfool.com

- **Nasdaq Stock Market**
  www.nasdaq.com

- **National Futures Association**
  www.nfa.futures.org

- **North American Securities Administrators Association**
  www.nasaa.org

■ Seeking Alpha
www.seekingalpha.com

■ TDAmeritrade
www.tdameritrade.com

■ The Street
www.thestreet.com

■ Wall Street Journal
www.wsj.com

■ Wall Street Oasis
www.wallstreetoasis.com

■ Wealthfront
www.wealthfront.com

■ Wharton School
www.wharton.upenn.edu